God Bless Tav,
Tracey Elliot R.

Photographs © Tracey Elliot-Reep
Designed and published by Tracey Elliot-Reep
Shilstone Rocks, Widecombe-in-the-Moor,
Devon, TQ13 7TF, England
www.traceyelliotreep.com

ISBN 0 9538231-2-1

Printed in England by Alpine Press
Station Road, Kings Langley,
Hertfordshire WD4 8LF

Foreward from the Duchy of Cornwall

One of the most enduring emblems of Dartmoor is the Dartmoor pony.

As this delightful book explains, ponies have roamed the Moor for thousands of years. Their ruggedness, reliability, good nature and freedom are captured in these photographs and embody for many much of what is so special about their history and their habitat. Tracey Elliot-Reep records how man has worked with Dartmoor ponies over centuries to meet the needs of the day whether as a beast of burden or, as more often the case today, simply for pleasure and enjoyment and maintaining the environment.

The Duchy of Cornwall is proud to be part of the Dartmoor Pony Moorland Scheme and I am delighted that these, and other initiatives, are working to safeguard the future of this most important asset of Dartmoor life and helping to ensure that a healthy herd of Dartmoor ponies will continue to play a part in maintaining the essence of Dartmoor's landscape.

This book 'A Celebration of the Dartmoor Pony' plays a special part in reminding us why the management and preservation of the stock is so importan

Bertie Ross
Secretary and Keeper of the Records, Duchy of Co
July 2004

Dartmoor, an area of 368 sq miles (954 sq km), is the largest and wildest area of open country in the south of England. It is one of the 11 National Parks of England and Wales and is largely of granite which is very evident with its numerous tors.

"The Dartmoor pony is the emblem of the Dartmoor National Park Authority and for many is associated with the National Park. The ponies on Dartmoor are an integral part of the landscape and many visitors to the National Park come specifically to see these animals in their natural environment. The healthy survival of the Dartmoor pony on the moor is in the minds of many people whose lives are touched by their presence." DNPA

All the ponies seen roaming freely on the Dartmoor commons belong to farmers who can identify their animal by ear tags, coat branding or other marks. These farmers have grazing rights, which allow them to keep limited numbers of sheep, cattle and ponies on certain areas of the moor. If these commons rights were not exercised and stock ceased to graze on the vegetation Dartmoor would soon become an impenetrable wilderness.

Shilstone Rocks D-Day with Duchy Scheme mares

Ponies have roamed Dartmoor for thousands of years. Approximately 3,500 years ago the horse became common in Europe. The earliest evidence of ponies' hoofprints dating back to 2000 B.C. were found during excavations on South West Dartmoor in the 1970s. More recent archeological finds elsewhere in the country suggest that Roman chariots were pulled by ponies similar in size to the Dartmoor pony.

The first written record of ponies on Dartmoor occurs in AD 1012, with a reference to the 'Wild horses' of Ashburton, owned by the Bishop of Crediton. Three 'unbroken' mares are mentioned in the Domesday book entry for Cornwood (1086). In 1535, in an attempt to improve horses throughout the country, Henry VIII decreed that stallions under 13 hands high should not be used for breeding (fine 40 shillings) but the remote hill ponies seemed to have escaped the edict. Early manorial records indicate that, as today, many ponies remained unbroken, but all were branded and usually ear-marked.

Early tin workers used them as pack ponies to bring tin ingots off the moor to be assayed (weighed and valued) at the Stannary towns of Ashburton, Tavistock, Chagford and Plympton. After the tin mining era, while some ponies were left to roam free on the moor, others were used for work on the farms, mainly shepherding and as driving ponies to take the family to market and to church.

Over the centuries a variety of stallions have been run on Dartmoor depending on the demand at the time. At one time a pack pony was required and the native pony was crossed with roadsters, a bigger type of pony. Then demand came for polo ponies so Thoroughbreds, Arabs, Fells and New Forests were used. In the coal mining era, Shetlands were brought down from the north and crossed with the Dartmoor ponies to produce smaller ponies to pull wagons from the coal face. Some of these were stabled underground and never saw the light of day after their arrival at the pit. Ponies were also used to pull wagons above ground on Dartmoor. In the mid 1800s Dartmoor was the main source of granite in Britain and at Haytor there are the remains of a granite railway that transported granite down to the quayside at Teigngrace and then on to the coast by canal. Old London Bridge was built from Haytor granite.

Tom Thumb

Ernie Worth © David German

Ernie Worth © David German

The Dartmoor pony has always been very versatile.
Right: Ernie Worth used to milk cows and for forty years do a delivery
round in Princetown with his pony. The same pony was used in the
afternoon to gather sheep, pull the hay cutters and get it into ricks using
the wooden sweeps at Peat Cott and Castle Farm.
     In medieval times the most common method of transporting
goods across Dartmoor was the packhorse which used to cross the many
rivers on the moor via the clapper bridges similar to this one at Postbridge.

Polo became a popular sport towards the later half of the 19th century as army officers returned from India where the game originated. In 1917 H.R.H. The Prince of Wales founded the Duchy Stud at Tor Royal (near Princetown) to breed suitable ponies for the game. The small, tough and sure footed Dartmoor Pony provided excellent foundation stock. In 1893 the National Pony Society was formed which laid down standards for each of the nine native pony breeds of the United Kingdom. The Dartmoor Pony Society was formed in 1925 and has continued to ensure the quality of this registered rare breed and to preserve the indigenous pony both on and off the moor.

The Dartmoor pony has a very kind nature and is an ideal pony for children. With their careful movement they are wonderful schoolmasters for young children and also make excellent Pony Club mounts and driving ponies as they are level headed, able and willing. Having strong build, limb and bone they can also accommodate a small adult quite easily.

Dartmoors have been exported worldwide, including to the U.S.A., France, Germany, Holland, Sweden, Norway, Malta, Austria, Australia, Falkland Islands, Canada, Denmark, Switzerland and the United Arab Emirates. Many of these countries have thriving Dartmoor Pony Societies.

Shilstone Rocks Panache and Windswept

Shilstone Rocks WarLord

Breed Standard of the Dartmoor Pony

Height: Not exceeding 12.2 hands high (127cms)

Colour: Bay, brown, black, grey, chestnut, roan. Piebalds and skewbalds are not allowed. Excessive white markings are disliked and discouraged.

Head & Neck: The head should be small with large kindly eyes and small alert ears. It should be well set on a good neck of medium length. The throat and jaws should be fine and showing no signs of coarseness or throatiness. Stallions have a moderate crest.

Shoulders: Good shoulders are most important. They should be well laid back and sloping, but not too fine at the withers.

Loin & Hindquarters: Strong and well covered with muscle. The hindquarters should be of medium length and neither level nor steeply sloping. The tail is well set up.

Limbs: The hocks should be well let down with plenty of length from hip to hock, clean cut and with plenty of bone below the hock. They should have a strong second thigh. They should not be 'sickled' or 'cow-hocked'.

Movement: Low straight coming from the shoulder with good hock action but without exaggeration.

General: The mane and tail should be full and flowing.

The same pure bred mare wintering out on Dartmoor (above) and the same year (below) a champion in show condition.

Shilstone Rocks Drizzle

Shistone Rocks Snowbird,
Another Bunch and Windswept

Left: Heavily in foal mares
Right: Mare with her young foal

Most foals are born between April and July.
Mares will carry their foals for an average of 333 days
(just over 11 months) although fillies tend to be born a
day or two before colts. During the last three months
before foaling the body-weight of the foal foetus increases
by two-thirds.

Shilstone Rocks Whirlwind and Atlantic Ocean

The foal starts breathing when the navel cord is parted and the oxygen and nutrition from the mare ceases. The mare will lick the mucus off its coat conscientiously from head to feet, and rub it with her muzzle which stimulates the circulation and helps its coat to dry . She then pushes her foal to and fro to encourage it to stand up and shortly it will instinctively find its way to the udder to drink the important colostrum (first) milk.

Shilstone Rocks Flamenco and Fiesta

The foals enjoy the spring and summer with their mothers and are usually weaned at five or six months.
The foals body weight doubles in the first couple of months and it grows 80% of its height in its first year.

Shilstone Rocks mares and foals

With the flush of spring grass in the valley pastures, the ponies exchange their thick winter coats for sleek shiny ones.

Dartmoor ponies are uniquely suited to life on
the moor. Gorse and brambles are an important
part of the ponies' diet, especially in winter.
Right: Traditional ponies on the moor.

The colours of the traditional and pure bred Dartmoor pony range from bay,
brown, black, grey (white), chestnut and roan. Piebalds (black and white)
and skewbalds (brown and white) are crossbreds, usually part Shetlands

Shilstone Rocks Freefall and Freedom

The ponies that can be seen grazing Dartmoor can vary widely in value. From the registered pure bred that may win Horse of the Year Show to the poorly crossed breeds that all too often fail to reach the minimum sale value at the autumn pony sales. In between are the traditional moorland ponies that some farmers have bred true to type for generations and which provide an important gene pool to ensure a secure future for the Dartmoor pony.

Above left: A pure bred Dartmoor
Middle: Crossbred.
Left: Shetland ponies.
Right: Traditional type ponies with one
        coloured crossbred.

Ponies in the Duchy Newtake Scheme

Dartmoor Pony Moorland Scheme

It is believed that in the early 1950s, there were around 30,000 ponies on Dartmoor. Now there are fewer than 2,000, and the pedigree pony is officially classed as 'vulnerable' by the Rare Breeds Survival Trust.

The Dartmoor Pony Moorland Scheme was introduced in 1988 by the Duchy of Cornwall and the Dartmoor Pony Society to halt the decline and is supported by the Dartmoor National Park Authority.

Owners of suitable mares living on Dartmoor are invited to put them into a moorland enclosure (known as a 'newtake') with pedigree stallions from 1st May to 1st October each year. The young ponies bred in the newtakes spend the winters on less exposed National Trust sites, where their grazing is encouraging the return of rare wild flowers, plants and the virtually extinct Large Blue Butterfly.

All mares are inspected by the Dartmoor Pony Society's own inspectors, and are branded if accepted. They are accommodated free of charge, and an incentive payment is made to their owners. All foals born from the scheme must be inspected, and if approved, they are registered with the Dartmoor Pony Society.

Since the scheme began several hundred foals have been born. Some colts have fulfilled one of the aims of the scheme by going back onto the open moor as working stallions and several fillies when shown, have won and been placed at county shows.

Shilstone Rocks Sweet Fury, Sweet Pea, Snowfall and Snowberry

Dartmoor pony colts above Widecombe-in-the-Moor.

Peps Ebenezer and Shilstone Rocks WarLord

Autumn Drifts

n late September and early October the local farmers who keep ponies on the moor round up the herds of ponies off their particular common. On foot and mounted on horses and quad bikes they herd the ponies into a convenient small field or ard, where they are then sorted into groups according to ownership.

After drifting the ponies the farmers decide which ones to sell, and return the rest to the moor until the following year. llegedly the majority were sold for meat but some of the ponies sold will go to be pets and children's riding ponies.

Pony drifting at Great Dunstone Farm

Hair accessories!

The Future of the Dartmoor Pony

In the past there have been many schemes to help the pony on the moor, including the Dartmoor National Park Authority Mare Scheme for traditional types and more recently, together with the Dartmoor Commoners' Council, the Stallion Approval Scheme. This included stallions of any breed being approved as healthy, hardy and of good confirmation before being allowed onto the commons.

The Hill Pony Society supports any type or breed of pony which come off Dartmoor.

The Dartmoor Pony Society along with the Duchy of Cornwall are trying to preserve the traditional indigenous Dartmoor pony, which obviously cannot be found breeding in its own environment anywhere else in the world.

A herd of registered pedigree Dartmoors winter out at over 1000 feet on the moor. The reflective collars ensure their safety when straying near roads at night.

The intention of this book is to bring a wider awareness of this unique native pony, and the need to preserve them for future generations.

Tracey Elliot-Reep

Tracey at 2 years on Jurston Maystorm with two sisters

Tracey's mother Elizabeth Newbolt-Young with Shilstone Rocks HeyDay

Tracey aged 5 with Shilstone Rocks Windswept I

I was one of five sisters who all grew up riding Dartmoor ponies on our mother's Shilstone Rocks Stud farm near Widecombe on Dartmoor. I can't remember when I first started riding but I do remember charging around freely on the ponies being a cowboy one minute and then an Indian bareback with a bow and arrow the next! One of the most memorable moments of my childhood was, when a bay Dartmoor pony wrapped in brown paper arrived in the kitchen on my birthday!

My love of these ponies comes from my mother Elizabeth who has dedicated her life to breeding and supporting the survival of the Dartmoor pony. As a child growing up near Chagford, she would often skip school to roam with the ponies on the moor. "There was one brown mare called Date Palm," she recalls," who I drove into the garden and into the chicken house and got on her back. She never seemed to mind!"

Since the Shilstone Rocks Stud was established in 1958 the ponies have been exported around the world. They have won Sire, Mare and Stallion of the year, Inter-Breed Ridden and In Hand Championships, have qualified for Olympia and Horse of the Year Show and have won and been highly placed in the finals of these prestigious events.

This selected portfolio of photographs of the Dartmoor ponies comes from endless hours of enjoyment with the ponies at Shilstone Rocks and on the moor.

www.dartmoor-ponies.co.uk
www.TraceyElliotReep.com